A FIRST LOOK AT
**AMERICA'S
PRESIDENTS**

LYNDON B. JOHNSON

The 36th President

by Kevin Blake

Consultant: David Greenberg
Professor of History
Rutgers University
New Brunswick, New Jersey

BEARPORT
PUBLISHING

New York, New York

Credits

Cover, Courtesy White House Historical Association (White House Collection); 4, Courtesy Lyndon B. Johnson Library; 5, Courtesy Lyndon B. Johnson Library; 6, © Mega Pixel/Shutterstock; 7T, Courtesy Lyndon B. Johnson Library; 7B, Courtesy Lyndon B. Johnson Library; 8L, © Diana Taliun/Shutterstock; 8R, Courtesy Lyndon B. Johnson Library; 9T, Courtesy Lyndon B. Johnson Library; 9B, Courtesy Lyndon B. Johnson Library; 10, Courtesy Lyndon B. Johnson Library; 11, Courtesy U.S. Senate; 12L, © AP Photo; 12R, © DSculptor/iStock; 13, Courtesy Lyndon B. Johnson Library, photo by Cecil B. Stoughton/White House; 14, © Evantravels/Shutterstock; 15T, Courtesy Lyndon B. Johnson Library; 15B, © Courtesy Duke University; 17T, © Consolidated Hector Robertin/picture-alliance/dpa/AP Images; 17B, © AP Photo/Frank C. Curtin; 18, Courtesy NASA; 19, Courtesy Lyndon B. Johnson Library; 22, Courtesy Library of Congress.

Publisher: Kenn Goin
Senior Editor: Joyce Tavolacci
Creative Director: Spencer Brinker
Production and Photo Research: Shoreline Publishing Group LLC

Library of Congress Cataloging-in-Publication Data

Names: Blake, Kevin, 1978– author.
Title: Lyndon B. Johnson : the 36th president / by Kevin Blake ; consultant, David Greenberg, Professor of History, Rutgers University.
Description: New Brunswick, New Jersey : Bearport Publishing, 2016. | Series: A first look at America's presidents | Includes bibliographical references and index. | Audience: Age 4–8.
Identifiers: LCCN 2015037936| ISBN 9781943553327 (library binding : alk. paper) | ISBN 1943553327 (library binding : alk. paper)
Subjects: LCSH: Johnson, Lyndon B. (Lyndon Baines), 1908-1973—Juvenile literature. | Presidents—United States—Biography—Juvenile literature. | United States—Politics and government—1963-1969—Juvenile literature.
Classification: LCC E847 .B56 2016 | DDC 973.923092—dc23
LC record available at http://lccn.loc.gov/2015037936

For more information, write to Bearport Publishing Company, Inc., 45 West 21st Street, Suite 3B, New York, New York 10010. Printed in the United States of America.

10 9 8 7 6 5 4 3 2 1

CONTENTS

Man of Action

Few presidents did more than Lyndon B. Johnson. He fought for **civil rights**. He passed laws that helped the poor and **elderly**. He made the air and water cleaner. Johnson also led the country during a terrible time—the Vietnam War.

Lyndon B. Johnson was also known as LBJ.

Lyndon B. Johnson was the 36th president. He served from 1963 to 1969.

A Boy from Texas

Lyndon Baines Johnson was born in 1908 in Texas. His family was poor. Lyndon knew that education could get him out of **poverty**. He worked hard and graduated high school two years early!

Lyndon was from a small town in Texas called Stonewall.

Lyndon as
a young boy

Lyndon grew up
around politics.
His father worked in
local government.

Lyndon's
father, Samuel

7

A Caring Teacher

After high school, Johnson became a teacher. He worked at a school for poor kids. Yet LBJ wanted to help even more people. So, he decided to work in government.

Johnson

LBJ with two other teachers

In 1934, LBJ married Claudia Taylor. Her nickname was Lady Bird.

LBJ and Lady Bird had two children, Lynda Bird and Luci Baines. They also had a dog named Little Beagle. All LBJs!

9

Master of the Senate

In 1937, LBJ was **elected** to the U.S. House of Representatives. He became friends with powerful politicians. Then, in 1948, he was elected to the U.S. Senate. LBJ was great at **persuading** people. He soon became one of the most influential senators in history.

Senator Johnson spent a lot of time getting to know other politicians. This helped him become a strong and respected leader.

The Senate and the House of Representatives are the two main groups that make laws in the United States.

In 1955, LBJ became the leader of the Senate. He helped pass laws that gave people more rights.

11

Vice President

In 1960, Senator John F. Kennedy ran for president. He chose LBJ to be his vice president. They won the election. Johnson worked hard as vice president. Then on November 22, 1963, something awful happened. President Kennedy was **assassinated**. LBJ was now the president.

Senators Kennedy and Johnson didn't always like each other. Yet they made a good team.

As vice president, LBJ headed the space program. He helped Americans explore outer space.

Vice President Johnson
becomes the new president
after Kennedy's assassination.

A Great Society

As president, LBJ focused on helping Americans. He passed two major civil rights laws for African Americans. LBJ also made sure that the poor and elderly could get medical care. He fought to give everyone access to education, too.

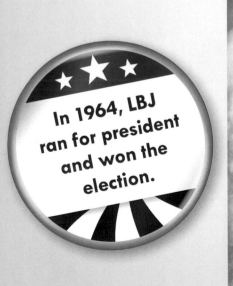

In 1964, LBJ ran for president and won the election.

President Johnson passed laws to keep the air and water clean.

For many years, African Americans didn't have the same rights as white Americans.

Martin Luther King, Jr.

Martin Luther King, Jr. looked on as LBJ signed an important civil rights law.

The Vietnam War

The greatest problem President Johnson faced was the Vietnam War (1954–1975). The war began after Vietnam split into two parts. In 1964, LBJ sent 500,000 American troops to fight for South Vietnam. Soon after, many people began to **oppose** the war. They **protested** in the streets.

The Vietnam War was fought between North Vietnam and South Vietnam. The United States fought on the side of South Vietnam.

Vietnam is located in Southeast Asia. Today, it's united as one country.

More than 58,000 Americans died during the long Vietnam War.

These protestors did not want the United States to fight in Vietnam.

END the WAR in VIET NAM

Remembering LBJ

In 1968, LBJ decided not to run again for president. He returned to Texas. In 1973, he died. Today, people remember him as a person who wanted to help others. Others criticize him for the way he handled the Vietnam War. Everyone can agree, however, that LBJ was an influential leader.

America's space program is based at the Johnson Space Center in Texas.

After leaving the White House, LBJ returned to his ranch in Texas.

TIMELINE

Here are some
major events from
Lyndon B. Johnson's life.

1908
Lyndon Baines
Johnson is born in
Stonewall, Texas.

1928–29
Johnson teaches
at a school in
Cotulla, Texas.

1937
Johnson is
elected to
the House of
Representatives.

1900	1910	1920	1930	1940

1934
LBJ marries
Claudia "Lady
Bird" Taylor.

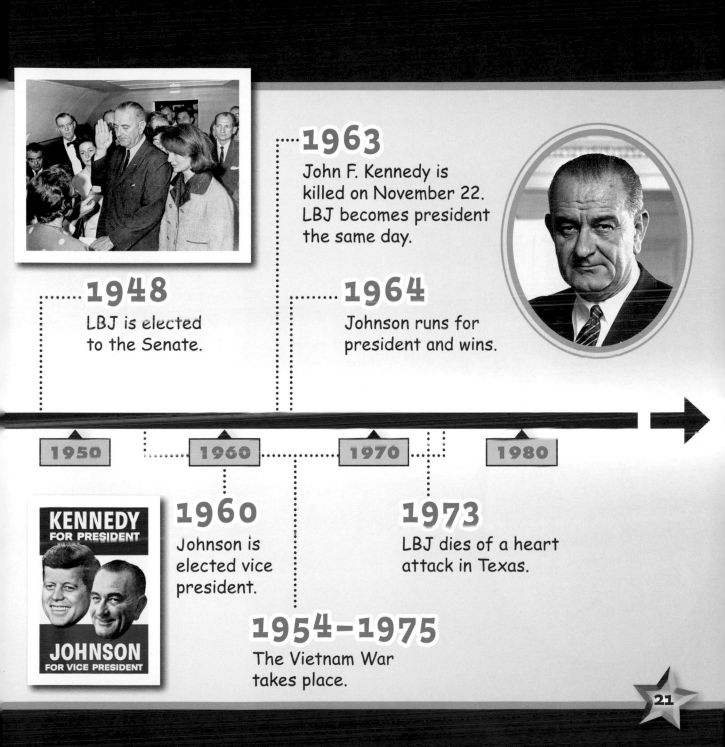

1963
John F. Kennedy is killed on November 22. LBJ becomes president the same day.

1948
LBJ is elected to the Senate.

1964
Johnson runs for president and wins.

1950

1960

1970

1980

KENNEDY
FOR PRESIDENT

JOHNSON
FOR VICE PRESIDENT

1960
Johnson is elected vice president.

1973
LBJ dies of a heart attack in Texas.

1954–1975
The Vietnam War takes place.

After President Kennedy was killed, LBJ was sworn in as president on an airplane called Air Force One.

"I am going to build the kind of nation that President Roosevelt hoped for, President Truman worked for, and President Kennedy died for."

"We have talked long enough in this country about equal rights. . . . It is time now to write the next chapter—and to write it in the books of law."

LBJ loved to eat mashed potatoes and canned green peas.

LBJ was very tall—he stood 6 feet 4 inches (1.9 m).

22

GLOSSARY

assassinated (uh-SASS-uh-nate-id) murdered

civil rights (SIV-uhl RITES) the rights everyone should have regardless of who they are

elderly (EL-dur-lee) old or aging people

elected (i-LEKT-uhd) chosen by voting

oppose (uh-POHZ) to be against something

persuading (pur-SWAYD-ing) trying to talk somebody into something

politics (POL-ih-tiks) having to do with running for and holding public office

poverty (POV-ur-tee) being poor

protested (PROH-test-uhd) to object to something by marching or by waving signs

Index

Read More

Gunderson, Megan M. *Lyndon B. Johnson: 36th President of the United States.* Edina, MN: ABDO (2009).

Mattern, Joanne. *Lady Bird Johnson (First Ladies).* Edina, MN: ABDO (2007).

Venezia, Mike. *Lyndon B. Johnson: Thirty-Sixth President 1963–1969 (Getting to Know the U.S. Presidents).* New York: Scholastic (2007).

Learn More Online

To learn more about Lyndon B. Johnson, visit **www.bearportpublishing.com/AmericasPresidents**

About the Author:
Kevin Blake writes books for kids. He lives in Providence, Rhode Island, with his wife, Melissa, and their son, Sam.